Robert Livingstone Stanton

Causes for national humiliation

A discourse delivered on the day of fasting, humiliation and prayer,

recommended by the President of the United States 1861

Robert Livingstone Stanton

Causes for national humiliation
A discourse delivered on the day of fasting, humiliation and prayer, recommended by the President of the United States 1861

ISBN/EAN: 9783337282974

Printed in Europe, USA, Canada, Australia, Japan

Cover: Foto ©ninafisch / pixelio.de

More available books at **www.hansebooks.com**

NATIONAL HUMILIATION:

A DISCOURSE,

DELIVERED ON THE DAY OF FASTING, HUMILIATION AND PRAYER,
RECOMMENDED BY THE PRESIDENT OF THE UNITED STATES,

SEPTEMBER 26, 1861.

By R. L. STANTON, D. D.,

PASTOR OF THE FIRST PRESBYTERIAN CHURCH, CHILLICOTHE, OHIO.

"Liberty and Union, now and forever, one and inseparable."—"Secession is Civil War."
Daniel Webster.

"The power, the authority and dignity of the Government ought to be maintained, and resistance put down at every hazard." *Henry Clay.*

"The Federal Union must and shall be preserved." *Andrew Jackson.*

"Say ye not, A Confederacy, to all them to whom this people shall say, A Confederacy; neither fear ye their fear, nor be afraid." *The Prophet Isaiah.*

CINCINNATI:
MOORE, WILSTACH, KEYS & CO., Printers,
25 WEST FOURTH STREET.
1861.

CORRESPONDENCE.

CHILLICOTHE, Oct. 8, 1861.

REV. R. L. STANTON, D. D.,

Dear Sir:—Believing that the sentiments of your discourse on the state of the Nation, delivered on the 26th ult., are eminently just, patriotic, and suited to the times, and that the interests of our suffering country would be promoted by their wider circulation, we respectfully urge you to give them publicity in a permanent form, and for that purpose we ask a copy for publication.

Yours respectfully,

O. T. REEVES,	THEODORE SHERER,
WILLIAM WADDLE,	JOS. SILL,
ORLAND SMITH,	DANIEL DUSTMAN,
ALEX'R RENICK,	SAM'L F. McCOY,
WM. FULLERTON,	HUMPHREY FULLERTON,
J. MADEIRA,	ANDREW CARLISLE,
E. H. ALLEN,	HENRY S. LEWIS.
BENJ. F. STONE,	NATHANIEL WILSON,
WM. B. FRANKLIN,	THOMAS MILLER,
T. S. GOODMAN, JR.,	F. CAMPBELL,
DIXON FULLERTON,	JAS. McLANDBURGH.

CHILLICOTHE, Oct. 9, 1861.

HON. O. T. REEVES, DR. WADDLE, COL. SMITH, and others:

Gentlemen:—Your note of the 8th inst., asking a copy of my Fast-Day Discourse for publication, is before me. I received a note of similar purport from many of you, dated on the day of the delivery of the discourse. To that I gave a negative answer, as I could not, just then, command the time to make a copy for the press within the period required for the immediate purpose in hand.

To your present note, I respond affirmatively and cheerfully; and the more so, that persons who had not the opportunity to hear the discourse delivered, some of whom have given their opinions upon it, may read it for themselves and judge accordingly.

For its "sentiments," which I am gratified meet your approbation, I made no apology in the pulpit, and I make none now. I have been too long in the ministry, and know too well what belongs to the duties of the office, to be in any manner of doubt respecting the propriety of such an utterance on such an occasion, or to be in the least disturbed by any comments which have been made. It has always been deemed the just province of the pulpit, on days set apart by the civil authorities for public Humiliation or Thanksgiving, to speak out freely and fully upon national affairs, in their moral and religious bearings; to speak of public measures and public men, when the facts furnish the warrant; to discuss any policy of the government, vitally affecting the social, moral and spiritual well-being of the people; and thus to direct the reflections as well as the devotions of those committed to our charge. This is the principle by which I was guided in my discourse of the 26th ult. It will be found that it has no political bearing other than this. In the admirable paper of Dr. Hodge, upon "The State of the Country," in the Princeton Review of January last, he pertinently remarks: "There are occasions when political questions rise into the sphere of morals and religion; when the rule for political action is to be sought, not in considerations of state policy, but in the law of God."

At no time in our history as a nation has the pulpit of all denominations been more united and distinguished for patriotic devotion, than during the seven years' war of the Old Revolution, though then, as now, there were a few exceptions. We are again in the midst of a revolution. As I have spoken of its character in this discourse, I need say nothing of it here. I can not, however, refrain from remarking, that it is the time for earnest words and prompt action, if we are to save for our children the heritage which has come down to us through a baptism of blood and a sacrifice of treasure from our fathers. Nor can I envy either the head or the heart of that man who calls himself an AMERICAN, whether native or naturalized, but have for such only deep commiseration, who does not see, in the simple issue now before the country, that it is his duty to sustain the Federal Government in putting down this unwarranted rebellion, by all the power of his manhood—by his purse, his prayers, and his sword.

Most respectfully,

Your fellow-citizen,

R. L. STANTON.

By the President of the United States.

———o———

A PROCLAMATION.

———o———

Whereas, A joint committee of both Houses of Congress has waited on the President of the United States, and requested him to recommend a day of public humiliation, prayer and fasting, to be observed by the people of the United States with religious solemnities, and the offering of fervent supplications to Almighty God for the safety and welfare of these States, his blessings on their arms, and a speedy restoration to peace; *and whereas*, it is fit and becoming in all people, at all times, to acknowledge and revere the supreme government of God, to bow in humble submission to His chastisements, to confess and deplore their sins and transgressions, in the full conviction that the fear of the Lord is the beginning of wisdom, and to pray with all fervency and contrition for the pardon of their past offences, and for a blessing upon their present and prospective actions; *and whereas*, when our beloved country, once, by the blessing of God, united, prosperous and happy, is now afflicted with factious and civil war, it is peculiarly fit for us to recognize the hand of God in this visitation, and, in sorrowful remembrance of our own faults and crimes, as a nation and as individuals, to humble ourselves before Him, and to pray for his mercy; to pray that we may be spared further punishment, though most justly deserved; that our arms may be blessed, and made effectual for the re-establishment of law, order and peace throughout our country, and that the inestimable boon of civil and religious liberty, earned, under His guidance and blessing, by the labors and sufferings of our fathers, may be restored in all its original excellency; Therefore I, Abraham Lincoln, President of the United States, do appoint the last Thursday in September next as a day of humiliation, prayer and fasting, for all the people of the nation, and I do earnestly recommend to the people, and especially to all ministers and teachers of religion, of all denominations, to all heads of families, to observe and keep that day, according to their several creeds and modes of worship, in all humility, and with all religious solemnity, to the end that the united prayer of the nation may ascend to the Throne of Grace, and bring down plentiful blessings upon our own country.

In testimony whereof, &c.

ABRAHAM LINCOLN.

By the President,

WILLIAM H. SEWARD, *Secretary of State.*

FAST-DAY DISCOURSE.

Psalms, 4: 5.

"Offer the sacrifices of thanksgiving; and put your trust in the Lord."

The proclamation of the President of the United States, just read, indicates the object for which this day has been set apart from secular pursuits to religious solemnities. We are convened in the house of God in obedience to the President's recommendation, and I trust we may engage in the services of the present hour in the true spirit of his most admirable proclamation.

Such a day as this has never before dawned upon our country. There are, probably, at this moment, throughout this nation, one million of men under arms, and half that number within forty miles of its capital. We take into this estimate the armies in the field, North and South, with the regiments in camp and in process of organization, and the Home Guards in the cities and towns; and including all these, a million may fall far short of the full number. Is not this a most astounding fact? Has it, to-day, any parallel? Have any of the empires of the Old World such a military array within them?

And how speedily has all this been accomplished! Six months ago, thirty thousand men made up the whole number, probably, of armed soldiers in our country, while the actual army of the United States was but a trifle over half that number. The people were engaged in their ordinary pursuits, every kind of business was unusually brisk, the fruits of the earth and the products of the commerce of the seas were never more abundant, the hum of industry was heard on every hand, and a high degree of general prosperity, with all the blessings of peace, was enjoyed by all classes of our countrymen.

But now, within a half-year, how changed! The earth is yielding her annual reward to the husbandman, and under the blessing of a bountiful Providence all the necessaries and comforts of life are bestowed in rich profusion still. But yet, every branch of business and trade is more or less paralyzed, scores of thousands are thrown out of employment, the largest capitalists in many of our commercial marts have become bankrupt, hundreds of merchant ships float lazily in the docks, workshops are closed, railroads are broken up, and the buzz of the spindle and the ring of the anvil are silent in the places of daily toil; while now, the most familiar sounds heard in the valleys and over the hills and prairies and amid all the cities and villages of our land, from the Atlantic to the Pacific, and from the Northern Lakes to the Southern Gulf, are the roll of the drum, the blast of the bugle, and the measured tramp of armed men going forth to the terrible havoc of war. Yes!—it is a reality, that war, grim, bloody, relentless war, has become the business of the country, supplanting the pursuits of peace, and engaging larger armies than were ever led by Napoleon and Wellington, or Alexander and Xerxes, or Cæsar and Hannibal, combined.

And wherefore this world-astounding transition—a change that eclipses in its suddenness and magnitude all the extravagance of romance and fable? Have the despots of the Old World entered into a solemn league and covenant to destroy the Model Republic? Have they, under their Holy Alliance, sent their fleets and armies to blot out our very name, that our national example shall no longer cause their thrones to tremble? And is it to resist a foreign invasion of combined Europe, that we have so readily laid aside the arts of peace, and have, in a single summer, become like the people of ancient Sparta, a nation of soldiers? Ah! would that it were so. Would that this were all that we are marshaled in battle array for—to meet the world in arms! We would rejoice to accept even that terrible issue for the alternative that is forced upon us. But we have not the privilege of the exchange. CIVIL WAR is the issue that is made; and it is this fearful visitation, as a judgment of God, which has called us to the house of prayer.

And while such a day as this has never before arisen upon our country—a day for public national humiliation, prayer, and fasting, occasioned by such intestine strife—no such spectacle as this land now presents has ever been witnessed since the world was made. This is no extravagance. History tells of nothing like it. If we choose to examine the entire past history or present condition of the world, comparing other nations with our own, a few months ago—with her more than thirty millions of people and her wide domain of empire, covering twenty degrees of latitude and fifty-five of longitude, the richest and most varied in soil and climate and productions ever watered by the rains of heaven; with her free and elective form of popular government, by universal suffrage; with commerce and manufactures which vie with the most forward nations of Europe; with inventive genius and mechanical skill which have made America the home of some of the grandest discoveries of the age; with a system of popular education superior to that of any other, which brings its blessings to the rich and poor alike; with religious institutions unparalleled for their influence and prevalence, benign and universal, and yet supported by the unconstrained good will of the people; in a word, with all the known appliances of a high civilization, which places ours in the front rank among the nations of the earth, in this age of rapid and amazing progress—and then, if we compare all this with what is presented to the world's eye to-day, as our condition, the whole nation armed in a bloody civil war, by which all this good to ourselves and its example to the world are fearfully imperiled, is it not stating the case in the simplest words of truth when we say that in no age of the world has such a spectacle ever before been witnessed?

But the question still presses, and from these very considerations still more urgently, *What are the causes* which have plunged such a people into an embittered war with one another, so that it should seem suitable for us to convene in the sanctuary, and as a nation come before the God of Nations in the ordinances of worship?

This question, justly considered, will bring our minds to the proper subjects of contemplation to-day, and may aid our hearts to proper feelings in view of them. The answer to this question presents itself in a two-fold light—causes arising from conflicting views and interests among the people themselves, as divided into the two great sections now at strife; and causes arising from the sins of the whole nation, which have justly provoked and brought down the judgments of God upon us, as war in all its forms, whatever may be its secondary causes, is always regarded in Scripture as a visitation of God upon nations for their offences against the principles he has laid down for their conduct.

It is highly proper for us to examine the causes involved in both branches of the subject. If we can view them justly, weighing their real merits, and can be suitably affected in heart by the view, and can be led to a right conduct thereby, we may, in our worship, enter into the true spirit of the first part of our text: "Offer the sacrifices of righteousness." And then, if we take a just view of the perils that are before this nation, and of the true source of its deliverance, as a christian people—however strong may be our reliance upon armies and munitions of war, and however earnestly we should as patriots support them, and as christians pray for their success—we shall be led to look beyond these mere means of safety, and obey the injunction of the second part of the text: "Put your trust in the Lord."

This text, as a whole, presents to my own mind, in its obvious suggestions, just those topics for thought and feeling which the appointed worship on this day of humiliation should beget. In endeavoring to lead your minds and hearts in these services, it is no affectation in me to say, that I feel utterly incompetent to do justice to the occasion, or the subjects on which I propose to dwell.

"Offer the sacrifices of righteousness; and put your trust in the Lord." The text is plain, and calls for little or no exposition. To "offer a sacrifice" to God, is as well understood under the Christian as it was under the Mosaic economy, and it is a duty which belongs to both. Then, it was the putting to death of an animal, and presenting it upon the altar; or the devoting of some other gift in the same way.

Now, it is a spiritual devotion to God, of the affections of the heart and the services of the life. To offer a "sacrifice of righteousness," was then, not the immolation of righteousness itself, but the presenting of a victim without blemish, typical of the Immaculate Lamb of God, with a penitent heart in the worshipper and a faith in the perfect righteousness of the promised Messiah. It is the same now, spiritually, and is the offering to God of holy affections and holy services, with penitence for sin, and faith in the obedience and sacrifice of Christ. To "put your trust in the Lord," is a phrase of the text meaning then, now, and at all times, substantially and spiritually the same thing.

Now, what application shall we make of this plain text to this day, and to the objects for which it is set apart?

God rules the world in righteousness, and he requires righteousness in mankind. "Clouds and darkness are round about him; righteousness and judgment are the habitation of his throne." He says to man : "Be ye holy, for I am holy." And he is only pleased with and favorable to men when they exhibit a character for righteousness: "Then shalt thou be pleased with the sacrifices of righteousness."

The same character which he requires in men individually, he demands of nations organically; of the people and their rulers; in the form and administration of government over and among themselves, respecting all classes and individuals, as citizens embraced in or others under the control of the State; and in all the intercourse of nations one with another. What is sin or righteousness in the individual, under the law of God, is such in the nation at large and organically, so far as these characteristics may apply to men and nations respectively. Hence we hear God saying : "It is an abomination to kings to commit wickedness; for the throne is established by righteousness." "Righteousness exalteth a nation; but sin is a reproach to any people."

And not only does God demand righteousness in men, but he punishes them when they do not exhibit it. This is written on every page of his word. He deals upon this principle with nations : "Thus saith the Lord unto this people, Thus have they loved to wander, they have not refrained their feet, therefore the Lord doth not accept them; he will now remember their iniquity, and visit their sins." And in order to deliver both men and nations from their sins, to induce humiliation and repentance, and to lead them to do the works of righteousness, he brings upon them his sore judgments: "When thy judgments are in the earth, the inhabitants of the world will learn righteousness." For this end, the minister of God is directed: "Cry aloud, spare not, lift up thy voice like a trumpet, and show my people their transgressions, and the house of Jacob their sins. Yet, they seek me daily, and delight to know my ways, as a nation that did righteousness."

Such, then, being God's character and administration—distinguished for righteousness, demanding it in nations as in men, visiting them with judgment for sin that he may punish and destroy them or bring them to righteousness through repentance, and as he at this moment is desolating our land with judgments to bring us as we would hope to see our sins and to repent of them and turn to righteousness, and not to destroy us—the duty before us to-day is a plain one. It is to inquire what have been our sins as a people which have provoked God's displeasure, to confess them, to humble ourselves and repent; and then to show forth, in place of the things wherein we have offended, a righteous conduct before heaven and the world. We shall in this manner, and we can in no other, "offer the sacrifices of righteousness."

Pursuing the plan already indicated, we may inquire, in reference to one branch of the causes of the judgments of God upon us as a nation,—

I. What are some of our National Sins, as committed against the Government of God over us?

I shall pass over this point with brevity, doing little more than naming some of our more prominent sins, in their special aspect toward God, for a two-fold reason, (1.) That only a few weeks ago, suggested by the day of humiliation and prayer set apart by the General Assembly of our church, I preached on this subject, specifying and dwelling at length on some of our prominent national offences; and (2.) That the other branch of the causes of God's judgments, as seen in our national strife, arising from conflicting views and interests of the people among themselves, divided into the two great sections now at war, receives, perhaps, as a moral question, suited for discussion in the pulpit, too little attention, and may, certainly, on this national day, with eminent propriety, engage our thoughts.

On the first branch of the subject—What are our national sins against God?—I will state those dwelt upon, on the occasion already named.

1. *For our varied national blessings*, exceeding, greatly, those of most or all other nations, *we have not been, as a people, grateful to God*, from whom cometh, to nations as to men, "every good and perfect gift." *Ingratitude* is the sin. But it has gone beyond the negative state. *Our blessings have been our vain boast*, as though we had procured them by our own power alone, likening us, as a people, to Nebuchadnezzar, who vauntingly said : " Is not this great Babylon that I have built for the house of the kingdom, by the might of my power, and for the honor of my majesty?"

2. *Worldly prosperity, chiefly material, has been the god of our idolatry.* Gain and gold we have worshipped, leading to unscrupulous means to obtain them, and trampling upon God's laws and institutions to gratify their inordinate love.

3. *Dishonoring as a nation and a government, the Sabbath*, systematically and habitually, in several things then specified, as, (1.) In our universal mail system, there being no plea for this but its supposed advantage to our material interests ; a plea that would, if well founded, open every workshop and counting room in the country, and drive the plow on every farm. No moral interest can be promoted by it, (nor material, in the end,) for it is always a detriment to cross God's law ; and his law is the same here for nations as for individuals, the exceptions in favor of labor on that day being those only of " necessity and mercy." (2.) It was then mentioned, too, as showing Sabbath desecration, that the present war had been fruitful in illustrations, as seen in transporting troops and fighting battles, (all which is wrong, unless stern necessity should plead for it,) leading to a painful realization of the trite remark, that " war knows no Sabbath." But in this matter a reform has taken place in the right quarter, under the order of General McClellan. This

order and its already manifest effects are ominous of good, and inspire the christian heart with hope and nerve the power of prayer.

These are the sins on which I then chiefly dwelt, their importance appearing more manifest, perhaps, from their full illustration than in a bare statement of them as now given. They do not by any means exhaust the catalogue. There are many others which are offensive to heaven which have covered the whole land, and which are closely inter-woven with our present civil strife. On some of these it would be profitable to dwell, and highly appropriate on the present occasion, as they have been long and eminently characteristic of us as a people.

I will, however, mention one of the most obvious of these national offences, and most fruitful of our present evils, and show, in some measure, how it works. It is *the making of political opinions the standard and test of moral principles and obligations*, and the acting out under them of the highest duties of the citizen.

This phase of our public life is illustrated in the iron-bound partyism which has so extensively prevailed. It is seen in the demands of party, laid upon the people under the weight of certain political dogmas, to put partisans into office, and then laid upon the men so elected to carry out the behests of party. We have been politically educated in this, almost from the foundation of our government to the present time. To go with our party, to stand upon our plat-form, to vote the party ticket, to applaud party measures, and to defend all the acts of our party when in power; these have been made the standard of moral obligation, in things political. The children of each generation have been taught them. They have grown up to manhood under them. They have gone to the ballot box under their influence. And the deadly fruit of this bitter seed we are now reaping.

But on this vital matter a better day has dawned. Whether its full meridian will be as bright and healthful as its genial morning is yet to be seen. But there is now at least one gleam of hope. It is that patriotism is supplant-ing party. It was a refreshing sentiment, uttered by the present Secretary of State in the Senate of the United States last winter, in his great speech for the Union—a man who is regarded as the father of the party now in power, yet in this utterance rising above all the trammels of party, and a sentiment judged by the result in the North to which he referred, as creditable to his sagacity as a statesman as to his patriotism as a man—that the time was at hand when all parties and party platforms would be swept away, and when the whole people would be united " to save the country in a party of the Union." His prediction is realized; and God be thanked that there is patriotism enough left among the masses of the people to rise above the shackles of party, at such a time as this.

Following out the corrupt principle to which I have referred—making party dogmas the moral test of political obligations—we find another illustration of it, fruitful of evil. It is the elevation of men to the high places of power, covered with both moral and political corruption. If men's political dogmas were right, if they were of the party, if they stood square upon the platform, even though that polygonal structure were so skilfully made that it had a front on every side to delude the simple, it was regarded as a moral duty to give them our suffrage. Even serious minded men—religious men—have been willing to vote for any party man, regularly nominated, though bankrupt in every moral principle relating to private or public life. I say not this of any particular party, but this has been too much a characteristic of our people, and we are now eating of the bitter fruit of our own doings.

Following out this dogma still further, and it comes to this—that the government, conducted by an administration elevated to power solely by party, must be conducted, in all its departments, upon partisan principles and for partisan objects. This is as well understood, and the obligation is as fully recognized, as though it were stipulated in the bond and ratified by oath and seal. Its patronage must be given to partisans. The judicial ermine in our highest court, even upon the shoulders of the chief justice, must adorn the partisan. Offices at home and abroad must be filled by partisans, for " to the victors belong the spoils." We have been represented among all the nations of the world upon this

principle. Drunkards, gamblers, and men who have disre-
garded all the sanctities of domestic life, have been honored
by the Republic which they have disgraced, at the Courts of
the despotisms of the Old World. If they have been repu-
diated by their constituents at home, it has only furnished
the reason why they should be commissioned abroad. The
government of this free Republic, through its places of honor
and emolument, has not been regarded as made for *the people*,
but for *politicians*, and as really so as the governments of
Europe have been regarded as made for the crowned heads
that administer them. This is the principle which has governed party conventions, and which, through the subtlety
and power of party organizations, has extensively governed
the ballot box.

These are but a few of the more palpable illustrations,
which start up on every hand, of the corrupt principle of
making partisan opinions and partisan action the test of the
obligation of the citizen, in the exercise of the right of suffrage, one of the very highest and most sacred of all his
public duties.

Can we marvel, then, that under such a recognized system
of political virtue we have become mournfully corrupt as a
nation, and that our offence is rank and smells to heaven?
Could it be possible, under the prevalence of such a principle, that any part of the body politic should escape demor-
alization? Prompted by such power, could any law of God
successfully withstand assault, if it should presume to stand
in the way of reaching partisan ends? Or could any interest
of humanity be safe, if challenged to such a contest? Can
we wonder, then, that under such a code of political action,
we should now be plunged into civil war? Can we not see,
in this, at least one of the causes, and that not the least
potent, of our present national strife?--that the section now
in revolt, which, through partisan organization, has managed
the government nearly from its origin, enjoying largely its
honors and emoluments in civil and military life, though an
extreme minority of the people, should now, through its political leaders, when they see the sceptre departing from their
hands forever, determine to overthrow the government by
an armed rebellion in several of the States? Are we sur-

prized at this? Yes! at this we *may* stand amazed—and so does the whole world—making all due allowance, too, for the personal and political corruption of human nature, when we scan the magnitude and determination of this bloody attempt to overturn the best government for the largest happiness of man, admitting all its defects of administration, upon which the sun has ever shone. I seriously doubt whether the corruption of *devils* is too deep to prevent *them* from standing aghast in all the caverns of hell, at this folly, this infatuation, this very· madness of wickedness, in the demagogues of the nation to effect this purpose! You may search all the records of history for a parallel, and you will not find it, for such an unwarranted and wide-spread rebellion.

And this brings me directly to state some of the causes in the other general branch of the subject, which have occasioned our present strife,—

II. CAUSES ARISING FROM CONFLICTING VIEWS AND INTERESTS OF THE PEOPLE, AS DIVIDED INTO THE TWO GREAT SECTIONS NOW AT WAR.

What are these causes? Some think they find them in the loss of political power and patronage sustained by the South, in the change of the Federal administration; or in their complaints about tariffs, and their desire for free trade; or in the doctrine of State rights, to which the South is attached, and to which they think the North has not due regard; or in their wish for a stronger government, in a limited monarchy, or at least with a privileged aristocrasy; or in a separate confederacy, by which they can regulate all these and a thousand other questions at pleasure, in despite of the power of the North, now grown great, and no longer controllable.

Some of these are without doubt proximate and even powerful causes. But there is one which underlies them all, the secret spring of the whole movement. *What is the great cause* which stimulates the South in its action, as given on the very best authority by the South itself? It is a cause which takes various shapes of statement, suited to the pressure of the moment, but always culminating in this—*to preserve, perpetuate, and extend the institution of Negro Slavery in this land.*

2

The object and limits of this discourse do not allow me to argue upon the right and wrong of this system. Nor is it necessary. I hold to the old doctrine of the fathers—a doctrine, till within a few years, universal in this country, in Church and State—that it is a system, politically, socially, and morally, evil and that continually, to both races concerned in it, and that it ought, just as soon as it will be for the interests of all concerned, to be brought to an end. I have in my library much of the literature of the South of modern days, on the subject of ·slavery, from the huge octavo to the smaller volume, periodicals, sermons, pamphlets, newspapers, from Cobb, and Bledsoe, and Smylie, and Palmer, and Thornwell, and many others. I have examined their arguments attentively, and some of these writers are men of master mind. If any person can make the worse appear the better reason it is they. I am not convinced by them; perhaps it is my fault. Besides this, I have lived where the system prevails, in the extreme South, in Mississippi and New Orleans, for the larger part of my professional life. I have seen it in city and country, at work and in recreation, upon the plantation and in the household, in the cabin and in the church, at home and abroad, and I am not aware that I have yet to learn anything new about American slavery as a system. And yet, I am free to say, that the more I have known of it, the longer I have lived among it, and the more I have read about it, the firmer is my conviction that the old doctrine of the fathers is correct, and that the modern doctrine of its divinity is another gospel and a pestilent heresy. This conviction is only the more strengthened, when I see that *the radical cause*, assigned by the South itself, for overthrowing the authority among them of the Federal Government, is to preserve, perpetuate, and extend the system in this fair land, until, perchance, the dream and boast of the late Secretary of State of the Southern Confederacy, in the Senate of the United States, shall be realized, that he would yet call the roll of his slaves at the foot of the Bunker Hill monument.

Does any one ask for the proof that this is the main cause which the South itself assigns for its attempted revolution? It is found, in one form or another, in the writings and speeches of their leading men in Church and State, and in the Constitution they have framed. Dr. Palmer is a representative man of the Southern Church, a native of South Carolina, and a resident of New-Orleans. In his Thanksgiving Discourse of last November, in urging the South to independent political action, he says it is her great providen-'tial mission to "conserve and perpetuate the system," and this is his grand argument for secession.* Alexander H. Stephens is a representative man among Southern statesmen. He rejoices in the establishment of the Southern Confederacy, because negro slavery is made the "corner stone" on which the edifice rests; and he deems it a worthy theme for their public self-gratulation, that theirs is the first great civilized nation which has rested on such a basis.† For this same purpose, they have modified their supreme organic law; and the most prominent of the changes made in their Constitution from the old one, is in the immunities and safeguards granted to the institution of slavery. The proof then is ample—they being witnesses—that this is the radical cause of their revolt, which underlies all others.

Granting, then, this to be the cause, what was there in the condition of the country, or in the action of the government, which could be deemed sufficient to justify the revolt, *even as viewed by themselves*, in order to secure the institution from supposed danger? In giving the answer to this question, I speak advisedly. I have read their most elaborate defences of the movement, from their public "Declaration of Independence," as they term it, to the utterances of their statesmen and divines. They do not plead any action of the Federal Government in justification, either in its Executive, Legislative, or Judicial Departments. When this revolt began, each department was under the control of the party with which the large majority of the South had always acted; and yet, it is against *this Government alone*—its Constitution, Laws, and authority—that the rebellion is waged. What, then, is the plea which they make? When their disquisitions are put into the crucible and reduced to their last analysis, it comes to this—THE APPREHENSION, pretended or real, that the administration coming into power, four months after the rebellion was inaugurated, would, or *might*, wage

* See Appendix, Note A.　　† See Appendix, Note B.

war upon, or exert its influence in some way against, the institution of slavery; and this, too, when all departments of the Government but the Executive, would still be in their own hands. This is the plea, and the whole of it, fairly stated, leading Southern men being the sworn witnesses. And this plea they urged, and acted upon, and filled the whole South with their sophistry to make out a case, when it was patent to all the world, that such a purpose in the party coming into power, was denied over and over again, in the most explicit terms, and in all the possible official forms known to the case, from the declarations of Conventions and the President elect down to all its leading public men ; and no tongue or pen was ever authorized to utter the contrary of these denials—to say nothing of the impassable impediments offered in the Constitution and Laws to any such action. And yet, they inaugurate this astounding, bloody revolution, against this mild and free Government of *the People*, in the face of all this testimony to disprove their imaginary *apprehension*—the only plea they venture to offer ! Was ever such an instance heard of, since rebellion and revolution were terms known in the vocabulary of man? *

And what would be, reasonably, their prospect of success in preserving the institution of slavery, should they succeed in establishing their Southern Government? The answer to this is best furnished in the sagacious words of an old Virginian spoken to me last winter, a man who has been in the Congress of the United States. "I am amazed," said he, in substance, "at the infatuation of Southern men, in their supposing they can save the institution of slavery by dissolving the Union. Why," said he, "the Constitution and the Union are what have made it controllable, profitable, and safe. It could not have lived to this day without them. If they dissolve the Union, I fear it will speedily come to an end and go down in violence and blood!" This is valuable testimony, and it accords with what is palpable to common observation. And this is one of the items in the account which induces the belief that the men who are leading on this movement are covered with judicial blindness, and that through this very blindness God may bring to an end that which they would preserve, illustrating also the heathen

* See Appendix, Note C.

proverb, that, " Whom the gods wish to destroy they first make mad."

In attempting to give color to the *apprehension* referred to, and in justification of the revolt by reason of it, it was said by the Southern leaders, that the present generation of the North have been for thirty years under a process of education which has at length totally abolitionized the people, that they are about to have control of the government, and that is what we fear at the South.

To none but the inebriate does the ground appear to be reeling. The change in sentiment with regard to slavery, is in the South rather than in the North. Forty-three years ago last May, the General Assembly of the Presbyterian Church put forth an elaborate paper on slavery. * It fairly represents what was then the general sentiment of the country, in the Church and the State, and in both sections of the Union. The paper was drawn up by Dr. Baxter of Virginia, and was adopted by the Assembly unanimously, every Southern and every Northern man voting for it. It is decidedly opposed to the system, and so strong in its statements that the South of to-day pronounce it an abolition document, and reject it with scorn. The present sentiment of the Presbyterian Church in the North, though now as ever opposed to slavery, is not unanimously accordant with the teachings of that document. The few among the people of the North who have gone to the utmost verge of opposition to the system—the ultra abolitionists, as they are termed—are more than overbalanced, in number and influence, by those holding views more conservative or proslavery, than the paper referred to ; while yet, now as then, and then as now, and always, the general sentiment of the North concerning the system, has been and is just what the general sentiment of the South was, until within a comparatively few years, viz :—that slavery was an evil to both races, political, social, moral, entire. The proof of this you will not ask me to give. The world knows it by heart.

While, then, the North stands on this platform to-day, while the evil of the system is the pole-star of her sentiment, the South has completely boxed the compass ; and now, with her people, the essential goodness and divinity of the system

* See Appendix, Note D.

and the relation of master and slave as such, constitute the
corner-stone of their so-called government, an axiom in their
political economy, the doctrine taught in their schools, and
the theology preached in their pulpits. *They* are reeling
and staggering under the intoxication of the teachings by
which they have been but too willingly drugged—and lo!
they look up and think the whole world but themselves is
turned upside down!

Precisely analogous to the change which has taken place
in the Southern mind under the teaching of some of her
divines, respecting the merits of the system of slavery, is the
change which has occurred there, under the lead of certain
of her statesmen, touching the relations of the Federal Government and the Federal Constitution to that system. By
all the political fathers, slavery was regarded as an evil, and
destined, sooner or later, to come to an end. And although
they made no provision in the Federal Constitution for its
termination—it being regarded as a State institution, to be
regulated, perpetuated, or ended, by State authority—yet,
that Constitution was formed by men who with great unanimity held such a sentiment. You do not ask me to stop
to give you the proof of this here. Every one who reads
knows it to be true. The Vice President of the Southern
Confederacy admits it, in one of his elaborate harangues,
made since the Southern revolt commenced.* Can it be
supposed, then, as a possible thing, that what has been
claimed for the Constitution as its original intent and meaning, in these latter days, is well founded?—that the Constitution carries slavery wherever it goes, into all the Territories of the land? One of the prime canons for the inter-
pretation of any written document, executed in good faith,
is, that it is to be construed according to the intended meaning of its authors, if that meaning can be ascertained. Tried
by this rule, was the Constitution intended to grant what
the South now claim upon the point in question? They
hold to the principle of strict construction. Do they find
this doctrine there taught? Passing by the well known
sentiments of the fathers upon slavery, if we wished to show

---

* An extract from this speech is given in Appendix, Note B.

how those viewed the Constitution who made it—and who should know what it was intended to grant, if not they?—and to show how their sons of each succeeding generation have viewed it until within a very few years past, it would only be necessary to note the fact, that thirteen several times since the origin of the government, beginning with the administration of General Washington and coming down to that of Mr. Polk, has the Congress of the United States deliberately exercised the power, by positive enactment of law, prohibiting, limiting, and circumscribing slavery, in some of the Territories of the common government.* The South, however, here as in regard to the merits of the system, have revolutionized their opinions, since they have enthroned and under the golden reign of the fibrous King; and now they claim, as the very letter and spirit of the supreme organic law, that it carries their system wherever the Constitution reaches. †

And just here, in a nut-shell, stripped of all the sophistry of special pleading, is the germ of the rebellion. The Southren leaders have insisted for the last few years, prompted and backed by the amazing profits of the great Southern staple, that the Government, Legislative, Judicial and Executive, should be administered according to their modern views,—new, and entirely unsupported by the Constitution,—and they have been wonderfully successful in carrying their point; until now within a twelvemonth, when they find a spirit waked up in the land, determined to resist these manifest aggressions, turn back the tide of sentiment which had well nigh revolutionized the Government, and restore the Constitution to its true intent and policy upon the platform of the fathers, they deliberately determine to break up the Government, even at the hazard of civil war! This is the judgment which will enter into the records of history, and this the verdict which will be universal with posterity. Was

---

*Though there is a slight inaccuracy here—not at all, however, affecting the argument—I prefer to let the language stand just as preached. The error consists in confounding later with earlier action. The "thirteen times" covers a period beginning previous to the adoption of the present Constitution. A sufficiently full exhibition of the facts may be found in the Appendix Note E.

† See Appendix, Note F.

there over a more barefaced and gigantic iniquity enacted under the light of the heavens?

It is plain to see from this what the South is fighting for. And now on the other hand, what is the North fighting for? It is told in a word. We are *aiming* to save the LIFE OF THE NATION, so ruthlessly attacked. Ours is a *defensive* warfare. We are seeking to maintain our honor, our glory, our good name, even our existence, among the nations of the earth. Did we not seriously attempt this—meeting their aggression of war by force of arms—we should certainly receive, and we should justly merit, the contempt of the world; and I am just as clear in the conviction that we should incur the displeasure of God!

I have now indicated what I deem to be the causes under the second branch of the subject—all culminating in one—for the present rebellion. They are quite sufficient to bring down upon us the sorest judgments of God, and in view of them we should be bowed in the very dust of humiliation. Let us in the next and last place,—

III. LOOK AT THE CONDUCT OF OUR PUBLIC MEN, AS EXHIBITING CRIMES FOR WHICH WE AS A NATION SUFFER, AND WHICH SHOULD CAUSE SHAME AND SORROW.

This is, most certainly, a point of the general subject which claims earnest attention; and I honestly confess, that, in the conduct it reveals in our public men, and the pleas they make to justify it, it presents to my own mind, the most profound matter for national humiliation and shame, before earth and heaven, that this day of humiliation suggests.

The public men of a nation, civil and military, are its property. Their greatness, and honor, and fame, belong to the nation. They are a part of its own glory. Or their imbecility, crimes, meanness and treachery, contribute to the shame of the nation, to its dishonor and reproach among mankind. These are but common and universally accepted truths. Tried by them, what is our national humiliation to-day, before all the earth! The time was when to be an "American citizen" was a better passport among men, than it once was to be a citizen of Rome; and the American name was far more dearly loved, if not feared, than was ever that of Rome. But for nearly a twelvemonth past, how has it

been cast out across the Atlantic, with sneers and contempt!
But it need not affect us so painfully that a revolution is
attempted, though even that were sufficient cause for shame,
considering our excellent form of government. Revolutions,
however, frequently occur in the world; but that this rebellion should have revealed such conduct in so many of our
public men, from the President of the United States down,
is matter for deep mortification and sorrow. It has no parallel, exhibiting such magnificent proportions, in the whole
history of the world, and is well nigh enough to make an
American ashamed of his country. The only redeeming fea-
ture of the case is, that the nation has now arisen like a giant
refreshed with sleep, and has determined to throw off her
lethargy, and to purge out this corruption by applying the
only remedy the disease admits.

Going back to last December, and what a picture did our
public men present! Petrified imbecility sat in the Presidential chair. Standing around it was schooled and chronic
corruption in nearly every post in the Cabinet. The vene-
rable Secretary of State was an honored exception. But in
the Treasury, in the War, in the Navy, and in the Interior
Departments, were men eating the bread and wearing the
official robes of the Government, men who had taken a solemn oath to support the Constitution, and yet men who for
years were using the knowledge, the facilities, the power,
which all the more unsuspectingly their official station gave
them, to undermine the Government, to overthrow the Constitution, to organize against it an armed rebellion, and—as
may appear when all the documents shall come out, now in
the possession of the Executive authority—to seize upon
the capital itself, to prevent the induction of an administration constitutionally elected, and to inaugurate a Rebel
Government in its very stead and place! Thanks, under
God, be to one man, that a part of this programme failed—
the Lieutenant General of the Army.

Now, can you find a counterpart to this conduct in public
men, in all your knowledge of history, considering the form
and character of our Government, and the blessings to the
people at large, which it secures? Was there ever such
thieving, and robbery, and perjury, and treachery to trust and

station—such a fitting combination of malice and meanness—
in such a cluster of the rulers of any people? coming, too,
from that section of the country which claims a monopoly of
all the honor and high-bearing and chivalry which the land
contains?—a section where so soon and so extensively this
high example set them at the capital was so faithfully copied
by the rulers and the people of several of the States?—and
while, moreover, they had not even yet, and did not for
months afterwards, claim, at least before the public, that they
were engaged in *revolution*, but were only enacting "se-ces-
sion," falling back upon their rights within the Constitution;
and that in seizing forts, arsenals, ships, mints, custom-
houses, and public money, they were only exercising a kind
and paternal care over the property and in behalf of the Federal Government, in its time of peculiar trial and need! Oh!
methinks there is in these familiar facts—so familiar and so
often repeated in the months which have followed that they
have lost their effect upon us—enough to call for a *forty* days'
season of fasting and humiliation. These were public men.
This is the nation's dishonor and shame.

And then, a little later, when State after State enacted
their paper secession, how rapidly followed the defection of
our public men, in both branches of the National Legislature,
utterly repudiating the solemn oath to support the Federal
Constitution which each member takes when entering upon
his public duties, and giving all the influence of their abilities
and station in aid of the rebellion. And what a mournful
spectacle was presented by the Army and Navy, when so
many men who had been distinguished in the service of the
country, could so readily turn false to their special oaths of
allegiance which the service requires, laying off this allegiance
and swearing fealty to the powers in revolt, with the ease of
changing one garment for another; and stopping not short
of taking up arms, as leaders of the rebel forces, against a
Government which had educated them, fed them, clothed
them, and given them all their honor and fame, and against
which not one of them could say he had any complaint!
Such full-ripened fruits of criminality are not the growth of
a night. They are the results of a corruption whose fester-
ing loathsomeness has been long and deeply seated in the

body politic. What the prophet said of individual man spiritually, we may apply to the nation at large both morally and
politically, when such men are its representatives; and it
shows how pressing is the need of national repentance, and a
"sacrifice of righteousness:" "The whole head is sick and
the whole heart faint; from the sole of the foot even unto
the head there is no soundness in it, but wounds, and bruises,
and putrifying sores; they have not been closed, neither
bound up, neither mollified with ointment."

But a reason can be given for any course of action. When
we search for the reasons by which these men justify their
defection, we find they are two—one of a public and the
other of a personal nature. The public one is, that State
allegiance is superior to National, or that there is no other
than State allegiance; therefore, these acts are justifiable and
even demanded. Consequently, when my State secedes, it
is my duty to follow it. That is the argument—brief, but
potential.

There is a delectable sublimation of political philosophy
in this, up to the heights of which no poor foreigner has yet
been able to aspire. When he comes from fatherland to
enjoy the blessings of our Republic, *he* takes an oath of allegiance to the *Federal* Government, and no other. He never
knows any other allegiance, in whatever part of the country
he chooses to live. No State in the Union administers such
an oath as a term of citizenship. It is a matter which
belongs wholly to the Federal Government. State allegiance,
to the ignoring of National, is a modern invention, to meet
the emergencies of disloyalty. The fathers knew nothing of
it. The peculiar benefits of this newly-discovered political
wisdom are reserved for those who are "to the manor born,"
making a distinction among citizens unknown and repugnant
to the genius of our system of government, the special pro-
duct of this age, and making what would be treason in those
born elsewhere, a high public virtue in the native-born
citizen. Did absurdity ever reach a higher pitch?

Among the most humiliating exhibitions to a looker-on,
connected with this question of allegiance, was to observe, as
it was my misfortune to do, one of the Senators from Virginia and another from Texas, stand in their places in the

Senate last winter, while holding their seats and under their
oaths as Senators, and make it their boast in the face of the
Senate that they owed no allegiance to any Government but
that of their respective States. And yet, they sat there day
after day, and deliberated and voted upon public measures,
aiding or defeating them by their votes, until the end of
the session. A Senator or a Representative, renews his oath
to support the Constitution at the beginning of each new
term to each respectively. Senator Mason had probably
taken that oath on the floor of the Senate at least three or
four times successively. He had then either discovered and
adopted the doctrine of State allegiance recently, or his base-
ness must stand without a gage. But whether the discovery
was recent or remote, these men were at one and the same
moment acting under their oaths to support the Constitution
while using their official power to destroy the Government,
and making an open boast of their infamy and casting defi-
ance in the teeth of their peers in the highest legislative hall
of the nation. Such men, who can deliberately and shame-
lessly in this manner officially trample upon their solemn
appeals to God—and in these things they are but representative men of a large class—are ready for any deeds of darkness. Is there not cause for humiliation in the conduct of
our public men? Were ever such things heard of before?
Was ever such forbearance shown? Any other Government
than ours would have suspended those men between earth
and heaven, on the day of these utterances, before the sun
went down.*

---

* The obligations of allegiance, and the rights and immunities of the citizen
under that allegiance, have hitherto been supposed to be correlatives. But
Southern chivalry has changed all that. To show how Senator Mason regards
the rights of the citizen, even under his pet doctrine of State allegiance, we
need only give an extract from his letter to the people of Virginia, published
in the *Winchester Virginian* just before the election in that State on the question
of her secession, prompted by certain inquiries which had been put to him.
We give an entire paragraph: "If it be asked, what are those to do who in
their consciences can not vote to separate Virginia from the United States?
the answer is simple and plain: honor and duty alike require that they should
not vote on the question; if they retain such opinions they must leave the
State." This is worthy of Austria. Talk about "honor," when uttering such
an opinion upon an *election!* Can any one believe that such a man has the
remotest conception of the sentiment of "honor," or the least regard for the
doctrine of "allegiance" whether State or National, or any manner of concern
for the rights of any body, when he can deliberately pen such a paragraph?
This is Virginia chivalry!

Such are the men who are leading on this rebellion. It is under the influence of such a doctrine that it is prosecuted. But it is no small consolation to us in helping on the present war, that this is one of the pestiferous heresies which will be forever put to rest.

Beyond this public reason is a personal one which influences many to renounce their allegiance to the Federal Government, and follow their respective States out of the Union. A particular State is the place of their birth. When it secedes they must go with it, wherever they may be residing. That is the argument. Or their relatives and friends are there; and hence go their sympathies with the cause, perhaps their active aid, or they go in person. Or, one may say, my wife was born there, and her relatives and friends are there; hence I must go. This is the personal argument.

This, in many cases, has sundered the bonds between officers of the Army and Navy and the Federal Government, has led them to repudiate their oaths and renounce their allegiance. Is not this a slender excuse by which to justify the crime of treason?—a narrow foundation on which to rear the superstructure of a stupendous rebellion against any government, and especially against such a government as ours? And yet this plea has satisfied thousands. It has been uttered in due form and published to the world. Besides officers of the government who have acted upon it, ministers of the Gospel have given up their charges at the North, and have gone to the States of their nativity, which have seceded; or they have gone because their relatives were there, or their wives came from there; thus giving, for such reasons, their countenance to the treason and rebellion of others, and enacting their own. Is not this, too, a cause for deep humiliation?

I am by no means oblivious to the power which ties of kindred may justly exert to draw relatives and friends together in times of peril. Nor would I for one moment causelessly frown upon these better feelings of our nature, though they should exhibit human weakness and sometimes lead astray. But there is a great and fatal error here of a moral bearing which needs correcting. I hear it upon the lips of men and women frequently. It involves a radical

moral principle, whose workings are doing much damage in
social life, and to the public welfare. It is something like
this : It seems to be taken for granted, in this public issue
of loyalty with treason, that a Southern man, because he is
a Southern man, is much less culpable for taking the Southern
side of this question, than a Northern man would be; and
therefore, it is expected as natural, extenuated, justified, that
a native-born Southerner, living in the North, should give
up his business and his home—if a clergyman, that he should
resign his charge—and go and cast in his lot with the South,
with his relatives and friends; whereas, it would be a greater
moral wrong for a Northern man to take this course in aid
of the South, simply because his friends are not found there.
Hence, too, we find deeper censure cast upon Northern men
who were residing at the South when this issue was joined,
and who have given in their adhesion to the Southern Government, than are cast upon men born there. "Shame on
them," says one, "that they should abet treason, for they
were born on Northern soil, and their friends are here."
And thus, the whole question of moral principle and moral
obligation, involved in this momentous issue, is made to turn,
either North or South, as the case may be, upon the mere
incidents of birth and relationship. Now, if these are your
views, you must revise them, or you do a damage to yourself
by indulging them, a damage to truth, to moral principle,
and to the public weal. The question here involved is simply
one of right and wrong. God has not constituted these
family relationships so as to allow us to make the affection
and sympathy which these ties beget the test of duty in such
a great issue as this, nor indeed the test of duty in any thing
else, morally considered. I have no right, nor am I under
any obligation, (though some persons seem strangely to suppose they are,) with the law and gospel of God before me,
to follow my State to perdition if she chooses to go there,
simply because I was born within her jurisdiction, nor to
follow her out of the Union for such a reason. Nor have I
any right, nor am I under any obligation, to follow my father
or mother, brother or sister, wife or child, in any course
involving right and wrong, simply because they are united
to me by the ties of blood. On this principle, why are they

not under quite as much obligation to come with me, as I am to go with them? Perhaps their worldly interests, their business relations, or something of the kind, will not admit of it. Is, then, this the principle on which we shall solve a great question of public duty? Must it turn upon a mere matter of personal convenience?

We may rest assured that God has made family ties for another purpose, and not to confuse the judgment and blind the conscience on questions of moral obligation. This whole matter of public duty is to be decided upon its own intrinsic merits, according to the principles involved in the case, and without regard to where a man was born, or where he lives, or whether he has a relative on earth. It is the duty of *man as a citizen*, as a member of the body politic, that is here concerned, and nothing more. He who does not acknowledge this has not learned the moral alphabet.

I can respect a man who differs from me, even radically, on a question which he claims to have examined and judged upon its merits, for I possess no infallibility. I can respect a Northern man *just as fully* as I can a Southern man, who may not agree with me upon the present issue of loyalty and treason—though he might name it differently—viewing, as I suppose he may, the whole case from his own peculiar stand point; though I must confess that with regard to both of them the case in my judgment is too plain to admit of but one opinion. But I can have very little respect for public men who suspend the question of their duty to the Government, and make the issue of loyalty and treason turn upon lines of latitude or family relationships. And I have felt especially ashamed of my brethren of the ministerial profession, when I have seen so many of them give up their charges at the North and turn their speedy feet to the South, and publish to the world the reason, substantially, that they were born in Virginia, or Georgia, or Carolina, and they must follow their State; or that their relatives are there, their sympathies are with them, and they must go where they lead!

If these men are children, or imbeciles—in their minority and irresponsible—and if they have wandered too far from home, and are overtaken in an unwary moment by an

unexpected storm, let them hie to their homes again, go back
to their guardians and to the arms of their mothers and
nurses for protection, and we will pray for their safe arrival
and that they may never wander more. But if they have
come to man's estate—if they have a commission from God
to stand in the pulpit and teach the people—then for the
credit of the ministry, for the honor of human nature, let
them not in a time of civil war, for reasons which ought to
shame boys of fifteen years of age, turn their backs upon
their country and join the standard of a bloody rebellion,
and meekly publish such reasons from their pulpits and give
them to the world. If ever devils laugh in hell, it is over
such a spectacle as this! Have we not, in the conduct of
public men, causes for national humiliation?

It is, indeed, upon the clergy of the South that a very
large share of the responsibility rests for the inauguration
of the revolution there in progress. I speak by the record,
and prove it from their own lips and pens. Would that
there were time to give you the evidence in detail, but there
is not. They claim for themselves the credit. It is freely
accorded to them by Southern statesmen. They were the
first to change their opinions and to proclaim the divinity of
slavery; the State has but followed in their wake. * They
took the lead in many instances, and in others early rallied
around the politicians of the South, in this rebellion ; and
on every hand it is claimed and conceded, that, without the
influence of the clergy, leading on the church, they could not
have succeeded in arousing the masses of the people. † If
the clergy had even stood aloof from the movement—if not
able to muster moral courage to oppose it—we might have
had for them some charity. But they threw themselves into
the van—and they glory in it. Dr. Palmer, one of the most
eloquent divines of the age, preached his famous secession
sermon in New-Orleans on the 29th of November, nearly
one full month before South Carolina seceded, and while as
yet the current of public opinion in the Crescent City was
against secession, as evidenced in Conventions there held
afterwards, and yet he mounted the very crest of the com-

* See Appendix, Note G.   † See Appendix, Note H.

ing wave and became there the King of the storm. Dr.
Thornwell wrote in December his elaborate defence of secession, and published it in January in the Southern Presbyterian Quarterly Review. This was regarded by politicians
as by far the ablest paper ever written on the subject; and
edition after edition was printed, as also of Dr. Palmer's
sermon, and sown broadcast through the South. *

What class of men, then, are the most guilty to-day for
this wicked rebellion? Among divines I name such men as
these. One holds the pen of a ready writer and wields the
sabre of a keen dialectitian. The other, for the eloquence
of impassioned declamation, has few equals in Church or
State. I name also the Right Reverend Bishop Polk, now
a Major General in the Southern army. Such men have a
different sphere of operation from that of the political demagogue among the rabble which make up the staple of mobs.
They sway by their talents, their social affinities, their moral
character, their ecclesiastical position, and their general influence, the best and the most influential part of the community. They have waved their magic wand and twined
these leading multitudes into the bloody path of rebellion.

On the same principle, who of all the statesmen of the
South bears off the palm of guilt for ensnaring large num-
bers of the best citizens in the meshes of treason? It is not
your hot-blooded Keitt, and your blustering Toombs, and
your cool and calculating Davis, though the latter has
always been a plotter of disunion. It is Alexander H.
Stephens. Nor let this provoke a smile. The foremost
statesman of the South for ability, and purity of private and
public life; up to a late period when his State was in her
tribulation, and while sitting in her Convention, a Union
man still; opposing with unanswerable logic before the
Georgia Legislature, last November, her secession, attribut-
ing her prosperity to the Union, and denying that there was
any cause for her leaving it; and yet, finally falling in with
the tide and becoming the most vigorous of the oarsmen.
These are the reasons why he occupies the unenviable position I have named. When finding the torrent irresistible,
he could, with becoming grace and as an honest man, have

* Extracts from both, Appendix A. and C.

3

bowed before the storm and retired to private life. But the glitter of office and power had too strong attractions even for him, and hence he soon turns up the second in position in their Government but the first in eminent ability, to become the leading orator for secession, to battle against his own former impregnable arguments, and to drag the better classes in the trail of his treason.

These are the men, if any in the land, who for their obliviousness to their moral obligations in this highest crime known against the State, and for their ability and success in plotting its overthrow, first of any richly deserve the halter. Is there not abundant cause for humiliation on account of the defection of our public men?

And is there not in the causeless inception and peculiar character as illustrated in the entire history and progress of this Southern movement, enough to stimulate the loyal to put down and punish such iniquity for the sake of this and coming generations?—quite enough, as put into the lips of one of ancient times, when he would avenge his own " wrongs,"

"To stir a fever in the blood of age,
And make the infant's sinews strong as steel?"

There have been two men in our history holding the second office within the gift of the people, who have been regarded as guilty of the crime of treason. One was Vice President under Jefferson, and has long since passed from the stage. The other is the grandson of the Attorney General in Jefferson's Cabinet, of an honored ancestry, of highly honorable and distinguished family connections now living, in the persons of several of the ablest divines in our own church, and himself now holding a seat in the Senate of the United States. Behold him to-day! under the lashings of a guilty conscience, fleeing like a thief in the night, from his home in his native State, our nearest Southern sister, that he may escape the vengeance of the law, and heading an armed band of marauders to make war upon his own people who have three several times by overwhelming majorities voted against secession, and to make war upon that Government which has lavished upon him its distinguished honors! His name will hereafter be linked with that of Burr, while that of Arnold will be forgotten in the comparison. Oh! is there not in these days, in the conduct of our public men. cause for deep humiliation! And can we find anything, by the most diligent search, on this day of prayer for our country, which is a more profound cause for public, national humiliation, shame, and sorrow, to ourselves as a people, and in the eyes of all the world?

Be assured, I have not drawn these pictures of public men in Church and State—dimly though they have been painted compared with the livid hues of the originals—from the love of an amateur artist. I deeply mourn that these things are true. But I have attempted to discharge a patriotic duty. My love of country is the prompting motive. We have too much at stake in this contest—the Church as well as the State—to stand upon any squeamishness of feeling or mincing of speech with regard to men. If any of you who hear me do not sympathize with these sentiments, all I have to say is, that you do not approach the remotest confines of comprehending the terrible turpitude of the crime wrapped up in the simple phrase—*treason and armed rebellion against the Government of the United States.* I have as dear friends in the South as any man. I know them and I know their country well. If I am charged with impaling them here, I may answer with the ancient Roman—It is not because I love Cæsar less, but Rome more.

And now, what is our duty? It is to stand by our Government in this contest for its life. Fond mothers must give their sons—doting wives their husbands—loving sisters their brothers—and not hold them back when their country calls at such a time as this, but bid them haste to the battle-field, to the field of glory and of death if need be, to save our country from death in a grave dug by treason's hand. Follow them there with your sympathies and your prayers, and sustain them in the fight, and look beyond them, even to God, for victory to their arms. And thus in the offering you make for your country, you shall fulfill the demands of our text: "Offer the sacrifices of righteousness, and put your trust in the Lord."

And do you ask with the Psalmist of old, "Oh! Lord, how long?" For how many months or years must I offer up this daily sacrifice upon the altar of my country? The answer is, until the strife shall be ended and the country saved. Better is it that the contest should continue for years, if need be, if in the end treason may effectually be put down, and the causes which have brought it on forever cured. If they are not, we shall have chronic war, breaking out into violence every few years, and our children and our children's children will be ashamed of our memory. But if we do our duty, they will rise up and call us blessed. If we do our duty— if the loyal men and women of this land perform their duties *faithfully*, and I believe they will—then, and you may mark my word for it, six months from this day of prayer will not pass, before the Federal armies will have possession of every important city, town and post, in the South, before that identical old "banner of beauty and of glory," shot down by rebel guns from the flagstaff of Sumter, shall again wave over its walls, and the stars and stripes be again unfurled over every fortress, and arsenal, and custom-house, in every Southern port. And as the gallant commander of the department of the West, shall approach the Mexican Gulf, and knock at the gates of the Crescent City, he will have no such contest for admission as Jackson had to save it, when he disputed the approach of Pakenham upon the plains of Chalmette, but the people will welcome the Pathfinder as their Deliverer, and like "the iron gate that led into the city" of Jerusalem when the Apostle Peter was escaping from prison, the gates of New Orleans will "open to him of their own accord."

But what if the strife shall continue longer? We are contending for liberty, for country, for posterity, for mankind, and if God in his providence so direct we will labor longer, and yield a cheerful submission to his will. We will adopt as our motto the beautiful sentiment of Whittier, the Quaker poet:

If, for the age to come, this hour
Of trial hath vicarious power,
And blest by Thee, our present pain
Be Liberty's eternal gain.
    Thy will be done !
Strike Thou, the Master, we Thy keys,
The anthem of the destinies !
The minor of Thy loftier strain :
Our hearts shall breathe the old refrain,
    THY WILL BE DONE !

APPENDIX.

NOTE A.—PAGE 19.

THE following extracts are from Dr. Palmer's discourse: "In determining our duty in this emergency, it is necessary that we should first ascertain the nature of the trust providentially committed to us. * * * If, then, the South is such a people, what, at this juncture, is their providential trust? I answer, that it is *to conserve and perpetuate the institution of domestic slavery as now existing.* * * * Without, therefore, determining the question of duty for future generations, I simply say, that for us, as now situated, the duty is plain, of conserving and transmitting the system of slavery, *with the freest scope for its natural development and extension.* * * * No man has thoughtfully watched the progress of this controversy without being convinced that the crisis must at length come. * * * The embarrassment has been, while dodging amidst constitutional forms, to make an issue that should be clear, simple, and tangible. Such an issue is at length presented in the result of the recent Presidential election. * * * For myself, I say, that under the rule which threatens us, *I throw off the yoke of this Union* as readily as did our ancestors the yoke of King George III, and for causes immeasurably stronger than those pleaded in their celebrated Declaration. * * * The decree has gone forth that the institution of Southern slavery shall be constrained within assigned limits Though nature and Providence should send forth its branches like the Banyan tree, to take root in congenial soil, here is a power superior to both, that says it shall wither and die within its own charmed circle. What say you to this, to whom this great providential trust of conserving slavery is assigned? * * * *It is this that makes the crisis.* Whether we will or not, this is the historic moment when the fate of this institution hangs suspended in the balance. * * * As it appears to me, the course to be pursued in this emergency, is that which has already been inaugurated. Let the people in all the Southern States, in solemn council assembled, *reclaim the powers they have delegated.* * * Let them pledge each other in sacred covenant to uphold and perpetuate what they cannot resign without dishonor and palpable ruin. Let them further take all the necessary steps looking to *separate and independent existence,* and initiate measures for forming a *new and homogeneous Confederacy.* Thus prepared for every contingency, let the crisis come."——"It establishes the nature and solemnity of our present trust, to preserve and transmit our existing system of domestic servitude. with the right, unchanged by man, to go and root itself wherever Providence and nature may carry it. This trust we will discharge in the face of the worst possible peril. Though war be the aggregation of all evils, yet should the madness of the hour appeal to the arbitration of the sword, we will not shrink even from the baptism of fire."

Thus the eloquent declaimer furnishes the proof of the position I have taken, and urges disunion at the hazard of civil war nearly one full month before the "secession" of his own native South Carolina—for the purpose of "conserving and transmitting the system of slavery with the freest scope for its *natural development and extension.*"

Note B.—Page 19.

The Hon. Alexander H. Stephens, Vice President of the "Confederate States," in a speech at Savannah, March 21, 1861, as reported for the *Savannah Republican*, uses the following language:

"The new Constitution has put at rest, *forever,* all the agitating questions relating to our peculiar institutions—African Slavery as it exists amongst us—the proper *status* of the negro in our form of civilization. This was *the immediate cause* of the late rupture and present revolution. JEFFERSON, in his forecast, had anticipated this, as the '*rock upon which the old Union would split.*' *He was right.* What was conjecture with him, is now a realized fact. But whether he fully comprehended the great truth upon which that rock *stood and stands,* may be doubted. *The prevailing ideas entertained by him and most of the leading statesmen at the time of the formation of the old Constitution, were that the enslavement of the African was in violation of the laws of nature; that it was wrong in principle, socially, morally, and politically.* It was an evil they knew not well how to deal with, but the general opinion of the men of that day, was that some how or other, in the order of Providence, the institution would be evanescent and pass away. This idea, though not incorporated in the Constitution, WAS THE PREVAILING IDEA AT THE TIME. The Constitution, it is true, secured every essential guaranty to the institution while it should last, and hence no argument can be justly used against the Constitutional guarantees thus secured, because of the common sentiment of the day. *These ideas, however, were fundamentally wrong.* They rested upon the assumption of the equality of races. This was an error. It was a sandy foundation, and the idea of a Government built upon it, when 'storm came and wind blew, it *fell.*' Our new Government is founded upon exactly the opposite idea; its foundations are laid, its corner-stone rests, upon the great truth that the negro is not equal to the white man; that Slavery—subordination to the superior race—is his natural and moral condition. This, our new Government, is the first, in the history of the world, based upon this great physical, philosophical and moral truth."

Note C.—Page 20.

The following are extracts from Dr. Thornwell's celebrated article on the "State of the Country," in defence of secession, as published in the *Southern Presbyterian Review*, (a quarterly,) in January, 1861, showing that the *cause* of the rebellion, was the APPREHENSION of "something" to result to the institution of slavery from the election of Mr. Lincoln to the Presidency. Speaking of the action of the South Carolina Convention, he says: "The presumption clearly is, that there is something in the attitude of the Government which PORTENDS danger and demands resistance. There must be a cause for this intense and pervading sense of injustice and injury. * * The real cause of the intense excitement of the South, is not vain dreams of national glory in a separate Confederacy, nor the love of the filthy lucre of the African slave trade; it is the profound conviction that the Constitution, *in its relations to slavery*, has been virtually repealed; that the Government has assumed a new and dangerous attitude upon the subject; that we have, in short, new terms of union submitted to our acceptance or rejection. Here lies the evil. The election of Lincoln, when properly interpreted, is nothing more nor less than a proposition to the South to consent to a Government, fundamentally different *upon the question of slavery*, from that which our fathers established. If this point can be made out, *secession becomes not only a right but a bounden duty.* * * If, therefore, the South is not prepared to see her institutions surrounded by enemies, and wither and decay under these hostile influences, if she means to cherish and protect them, it is her bounden duty to resist the revolution which threatens them with ruin. The triumph of the principles which Mr. Lincoln is pledged to carry out, is the death-knell of slavery. * * The principle is at work and enthroned in power, whose inevitable TENDENCY is to secure this result. Let us crush the serpent in the egg. * * Under these circumstances, we do not see how any man can question either the *righteousness or the necessity of secession.*"

As further proof of the cause assigned being founded in the APPREHENSION referred to, take the following from Dr. Palmer's elaborate paper entitled "A Vindication of Secession and the South," published in the *Southern Presbyterian Review*, (a quarterly,) in April last, in reply to an article in the Danville Review by Dr. Breckinridge, of Kentucky:

"It betrays a want of statesmanship to overlook the *real causes* of a great popular movement, and to base a political remedy upon motives which are purely fanciful. Why will not Kentucky and the world believe the constant averment of the seceding South, that she has acted under the conviction of an *amazing peril*, and from a sense of compelling justice? Through nearly a half a century a party has been struggling for political rule, in sworn hostility to that institution upon which the life and being of the South depend. It has grown through all opposition, until it has imbued the public mind of the North with a kindred, though somewhat restrained, abhorrence of slavery. It has laid hold upon all parties as instruments of its will; and now at length, subordinating the Republicans as its pliant tool, it has throned itself upon the chair of State, and speaks with the authority of law. We need not go through all the details of a long and too familiar story, and recite the utterances and disclose the platforms of the dominant party now represented in the occupancy of the White House. What was the South to do? Submission at this stage would have been submission forever; and since this was impossible without the surrender of all that a people can hold dear—liberty, honor, and safety—she simply, and, as we think, with great dignity, withdrew from the disgraceful and destructive ASSOCIATION. Yet, while struggling thus for life itself, she is stigmatized by such a man as Dr. Breckinridge, with a base lust of power, or peevishly resenting the loss of a political control which she can not hope to recover."

NOTE D.—PAGE 21.

The following is the paper of the General Assembly referred to:

§ 42. *Action of the Assembly of* 1818.

(*a*) "The following resolution was submitted to the General Assembly, viz: "*Resolved,* That a person who shall sell as a slave, a member of the Church, who shall be at the time in good standing in the Church and unwilling to be sold, acts inconsistently with the spirit of Christianity, and ought to be debarred from the communion of the Church.

"After considerable discussion, the subject was committed to Dr. Green, Dr. Baxter, and Mr. Burgess, to prepare a report to be adopted by the Assembly, embracing the object of the above resolution, and also expressing the opinion of the Assembly in general, as to slavery."—*Minutes,* 1818, p. 688.

[The report of the committee was unanimously adopted, and is as follows, viz.]

"The General Assembly of the Presbyterian Church, having taken into consideration the subject of slavery, think proper to make known their sentiments upon it to the Churches and people under their care.

(*b*) "We consider the voluntary enslaving of one portion of the human race by another, as a gross violation of the most precious and sacred rights of human nature; as utterly inconsistent with the law of God, which requires us to love our neighbor as ourselves, and as totally irreconcilable with the spirit and principles of the gospel of Christ, which enjoins that 'all things whatsoever ye would that men should do to you, do ye even so to them.' Slavery creates a paradox in the moral system; it exhibits rational, accountable, and immortal beings in such circumstances as scarcely to leave them the power of moral action. It exhibits them as dependent on the will of others, whether they shall receive religious instruction; whether they shall know and worship the true God; whether they shall enjoy the ordinances of the gospel; whether they shall perform the duties and cherish the endearments of husbands and wives, parents and children, neighbors and friends; whether they shall preserve their chastity and purity, or regard the dictates of justice and humanity. Such are some of the consequences of slavery—consequences not imaginary, but which connect themselves with its very existence. The evils to which the slave is always exposed often take place in fact, and in their very worst degree and form; and where all of them do not take place, as we rejoice to say in many instances, through the influence of the principles of humanity and religion on the mind of masters, they do not—still the slave is deprived of his natural right, degraded as a human being, and exposed to the danger of passing into the hands of a master who may inflict upon him all the hardships and injuries which inhumanity and avarice may suggest.

"From this view of the consequences resulting from the practice into which Christian people have most inconsistently fallen, of enslaving a portion of their brethren of mankind—for 'God hath made of one blood all nations of men to dwell on the face of the earth'—it is manifestly the duty of all Christians who enjoy the light of the present day, when the inconsistency of slavery, both with the dictates of humanity and religion, has been demonstrated, and is generally seen and acknowledged, to use their honest, earnest, and unwearied endeavors, to correct the errors of former times, and as speedily as possible to efface this blot on our holy religion, and to obtain the complete abolition of slavery throughout Christendom, and if possible throughout the world.

(c) "We rejoice that the Church to which we belong commenced as early as any other in this country, the good work of endeavoring to put an end to slavery, and that in the same work many of its members have ever since been, and now are, among the most active, vigorous and efficient laborers. We do, indeed, tenderly sympathize with those portions of our Church and our country where the evil of slavery has been entailed upon them; where a great, and the most virtuous part of the community abhor slavery, and wish its extermination as sincerely as any others—but where the number of slaves, their ignorance, and their vicious habits generally, render an immediate and universal emancipation inconsistent alike with the safety and happiness of the master and the slave. With those who are thus circumstanced, we repeat that we tenderly sympathize. At the same time, we earnestly exhort them to continue, and if possible, to increase their exertions to effect a total abolition of slavery. We exhort them to suffer no greater delay to take place in this most interesting concern, than a regard for the public welfare truly and indispensably demands.

(d) "As our country has inflicted a most grievous injury upon the unhappy Africans, by bringing them into slavery, we cannot indeed urge that we should add a second injury to the first, by emancipating them in such manner as that they will be likely to destroy themselves or others. But we do think that our country ought to be governed in this matter by no other consideration than an honest and impartial regard to the happiness of the injured party, uninfluenced by the expense or inconvenience which such a regard may involve. We, therefore, warn all who belong to our denomination of Christians, against unduly extending this plea of necessity; against making it a cover for the love and practice of slavery, or a pretence for not using efforts that are lawful and practicable, to extinguish this evil.

"And we, at the same time, exhort others to forbear harsh censures, and uncharitable reflections on their brethren, who unhappily live among slaves whom they cannot immediately set free; but who, at the same time, are really using all their influence, and all their endeavors, to bring them into a state of freedom, as soon as a door for it can be safely opened.

"Having thus expressed our views of slavery, and of the duty indispensably incumbent on all Christians to labor for its complete extinction, we proceed to recommend, and we do it with all the earnestness and solemnity which this momentous subject demands, a particular attention to the following points.

(e) "We recommend to all our people to patronize and encourage the Society lately formed, for colonizing in Africa, the land of their ancestors, the free people of color in our country. We hope that much good may result from the plans and efforts of this Society. And while we exceedingly rejoice to have witnessed its origin and organization among the holders of slaves, as giving an unequivocal pledge of their desires to deliver themselves and their country from the calamity of slavery; we hope that those portions of the American union, whose inhabitants are by a gracious providence more favorably circumstanced, will cordially, and liberally, and earnestly co-operate with their brethren, in bringing about the great end contemplated.

(f) "We recommend to all the members of our religious denomination, not only to permit, but to facilitate and encourage the instruction of their slaves in the principles and duties of the Christian religion; by granting them liberty to attend on the preaching of the gospel, when they have opportunity; by favoring the instruction of them in the Sabbath-school, wherever those schools can be formed; and by giving them all other proper advantages for acquiring the knowledge of their duty both to God and to man. We are perfectly satisfied that it is incumbent on all Christians to communicate religious instruction to those who are under their authority, so that the doing of this in the case before us, so far from operating, as some have apprehended that it might, as an incitement to insubordination and insurrection, would, on the contrary, operate as a most powerful means for the prevention of those evils.

(g) "We enjoin it on all Church Sessions and Presbyteries, under the care of this Assembly, to discountenance, and as far as possible to prevent all cruelty of whatever kind in the treatment of slaves; especially the cruelty of separating husband and wife, parents and children, and that which consists in selling slaves to those who will either themselves deprive these unhappy people of the blessings of the gospel, or who will transport them to places where the gospel is not proclaimed, or where it is forbidden to slaves to attend upon its institutions. And if it shall ever happen that a Christian professor in our communion shall sell a slave who is also in communion and good standing with our Church, contrary to his or her will and inclination, it ought immediately to claim the particular attention of the proper Church judicature; and unless there be such peculiar circumstances attending the case as can but seldom happen, it ought to be followed, without delay, by a suspension of the offender from all the privileges of the Church, till he repent, and make all the reparation in his power to the injured party."—*Minutes*, 1818, p. 692.

Note E.—Page 23

The action of the "powers that be," (and that *were*,) under one form or another, has been very explicit in all times of our history, showing how the "political fathers" regarded slavery in connection with our Government, how they "resolved" about it in Conventions and in the Continental Congress, and how they repeatedly legislated upon it respecting the Territories ; and some of these various acts date back earlier than the adoption of the present Constitution, earlier, therefore, than is intimated in the body of the Discourse, ("since the origin of the Government, beginning with the administration of General Washington, and coming down to that of Mr Polk,") and they bring out the following results : 1. That to prevent the further introduction of African slaves, to prohibit the further extension of the system of slavery, and even to secure its final abolition, were prominent objects of the Revolution which established our national independence. 2. That all the leading men of that day, with very rare exceptions, agreed in these views and objects. 3. That, including the action of the Continental Congress under the old Confederation, and the Congress of the United States under the present Constitution, there has been direct legislation at least thirteen times, prohibitory of Slavery in the Territories. 4. That this legislation comes down to as late a period as the administration of James K. Polk, a Southern President, who signed the bill organizing the Territory of Oregon, prohibiting Slavery north of 36 : 30 degrees North latitude. 5. That, therefore, the doctrine that the Constitution carries Slavery into the Territories of its own inherent force, is a modern notion,— *very* modern,— never dreamed of by the men who made it.

The proof of these points in detail, would be tedious. The following historical data may suffice.

1. The proof of the first point is explicit. The "American Archives" were published by order of Congress, and are authoritative. In regard to the people of VIRGINIA, it is said, in the fourth volume :

"At a meeting of freeholders and other inhabitants of the county of Culpepper, in Virginia, assembled at the Court House of said county, on Thursday the 7th of July, 1774, to consider the most *effective method to preserve the rights and liberties* of America. *Resolved*, That the *importing slaves* and convict servants is *injurious to this colony, as it obstructs the population of it with freemen and useful manufactories* ; *and that we will not buy any such slave or convict servant hereafter to be imported.*"

Resolutions to the same effect were passed in many other counties in Virginia, and other Southern provinces. The State Convention met in Williamsburgh on the 1st of August 1774, and passed the following : "*Resolved*, That we will neither ourselves import, nor purchase any slave or slaves imported by any other person, after the first day of November next, either from Africa, the West Indies, or any other place." Mr Jefferson sent to the State Convention a letter containing the following :

"For the most trifling reasons, and sometimes for no conceivable reason at all, his Majesty has rejected laws of the most salutary tendency. The abolition of domestic slavery is the greatest object of desire in these colonies, where it was unhappily introduced in their infant state. But *previous to the enfranchisement of the slaves* we have, it is necessary to exclude all further importations from Africa. Yet our repeated attempts to effect this by prohibitions, and by imposing duties which might amount to prohibition, have been hitherto defeated by his Majesty's negative. Thus preferring the immediate advantages of a few African Corsairs to the lasting interests of the American States, and to the *rights of human nature deeply wounded by this infamous master.*"

The Convention of NORTH CAROLINA met at Newbern on the 27th of August 1774, and passed the following : "*Resolved*, That we will not import any slave or slaves, or purchase any slave or slaves imported, or brought into the Provinces by others from any part of the world, after the first day of November next."

Other Colonial Conventions took similar action. The delegates from the various colonies met in Congress, at Philadelphia, Sept. 5, 1774. They formed a union of the Colonies, under what was termed, "Articles of Association." They adopted these Articles unanimously. They state as follows :

"We do for ourselves and the inhabitants of the several Colonies whom we represent, firmly agree and associate under the sacred ties of virtue, honor and love our country, as follows : "That we will *neither import nor purchase, any slave imported after the first day of December next*, after which time we will *wholly discontinue the slave trade*, and will neither be concerned in it ourselves, nor will we hire our vessels, nor sell our commodities and manufactures to those who are concerned in it.

"That a Committee be chosen in every county, city, and town, by those who are qualified to vote for Representatives in the Legislature, whose business it shall be to attentively observe the conduct of all persons touching this Association; and whenever it shall be made to appear to the satisfaction of a majority of any such Committee, that any person within the limits of their appointment has violated this Association, that such majority do forthwith cause the truth of the case to be published in the Gazette, to the end that all such *foes to the rights of British America* may be publicly known, and *universally contemned as the enemies of American Liberty*; and thenceforth we will respectively break off all dealings with him or her."

"And we do further agree and resolve that we will have no trade, commerce, dealings, or intercourse whatever with any colony or province in North America, which shall not accede to, or which shall hereafter violate this Association, but will hold them as *unworthy of the rights of freemen, and as inimical to the liberties of this country.* The foregoing Association, being determined upon by the Congress, was ordered to be subscribed by the several members thereof; and thereupon we have hereunto set our respective names accordingly.—In Congress, Philadelphia, Oct. 20, 1774."

The names of all the delegates from all the colonies represented were signed to these Articles. GEORGIA alone was not represented in the Congress. The people of that Colony, however, met in Convention on the 12th of Jan. 1775, and passed the following:

"We, therefore, the Representatives of the extensive district of Darien, in the colony of Georgia, having now assembled in Congress, by the authority and free choice of the inhabitants of said District, now freed from their fetters, do resolve: To *show to the world that we are not influenced by any contracted or interested motives, but a general philanthropy for all mankind of whatever climate, language, or complexion,* we hereby declare our disapprobation and *abhorrence* of the *unnatural practice of slavery* in America, (however the uncultivated state of our country, or other specious arguments may plead for it,) a *practice founded in injustice and cruelty and highly dangerous* to our liberties (as well as lives), *debasing part of our fellow creatures below men,* and is laying the basis of that liberty we contend for, (and which we pray the Almighty to continue to the latest posterity), upon a very wrong foundation. We therefore *resolve at all times to use our utmost endeavors for the manumission of our slaves* in this colony upon the most safe and equitable footing for the master and themselves."

The Revolutionary war commenced in April, 1775, only a few months after this general action upon slavery. As the men of that day had seen all their efforts to restrict slavery and the slave trade vetoed by the British crown, they were determined to throw off the incubus, even at the hazard of civil war. Hence this design, as the moving cause, is presented with peculiar prominence in the *original form* in which the Declaration of Independence was drawn up, and the efforts of "good King George" are thus painted: "He has waged cruel war against human nature itself, violating its most sacred rights of life and liberty in the persons of a distant people who never offended him, captivating and carrying them into slavery in another hemisphere, or to incur a miserable death in their transportation hither. This piratical warfare, the opprobrium of Infidel Powers, is the warfare of the Christian King of Great Britain. Determined to keep open a market where men should be bought and sold, he has prostituted his negative for suppressing every legislative attempt to prohibit or restrain this execrable commerce. And that this assemblage of horrors might want no fact of distinguishing die, he is now exciting those very people to rise in arms among us, and to purchase that liberty of which he has deprived them, by murdering the people on whom he also obtruded them; thus paying off former crimes committed against the liberties of one people, with crimes which he urges them to commit against the lives of another."

2. The proof of the second of the above points is found in the action already given, and in the writings of men too well known to be repeated here.

3. This point embraces a range of proof too tedious to be given at length. (1.) One vital fact, showing that immediately after Independence was gained, the Continental Congress designed to carry out in good faith the principle with regard to slavery for which the Revolution was waged, is seen in its action upon the *then entire territory possessed*, adopting the famous "Ordinance for the government of the Territory of the United States Northwest of the Ohio river," July 13th, 1787. Eight States were represented, and voted on this Ordinance, three now free, and five now slave, viz: free States, Massachusetts, New York, and New Jersey; slave States, Delaware, Virginia, North Carolina, South Carolina, and Georgia. Every State voted for the Ordinance, and also every member but one, Mr. Yates of New York. The 6th article says: "There shall be neither slavery nor involuntary servitude in the said territory, otherwise than in punishment of crimes whereof the party shall have been duly convicted." Thus, at that time, *the whole public domain, the entire territory*, of the Union, was devoted to freedom by a unanimous vote, save one, and that from a free State. This was before the adoption of the present Constitution. (2.) The Federal Constitution was adopted in the same year, and in the Convention which framed it were many of the same men who in the Continental Congress had so recently passed the "Ordinance" above cited. They put no clause into the Constitution restrictive of slavery in the *States* as it was wholly a *State* institution. And, most assuredly, entertaining the sentiments on slavery so palpably and recently shown by their public action, they could not have intended the Constitution *to protect* slavery upon any soil covered by the Constitution exclusively, whether territory then owned Northwest of the Ohio, or any territory which might afterwards be obtained. "When the Constitution was adopted," it is argued, "the Ordinance of 1787 was no longer of force." Be it so, and what then? The Constitution says nothing of that Ordinance, nor did the Convention act upon it. To make the most of it, if the Ordinance was superseded, it was on the ground only that the Constitution was the supreme law. How then stands the case? (3.) Why, it stands thus: The *Legislative* Department of the government settled the matter. One of the first acts of the first Congress, under the Constitution, (embracing, again, many men who had been in the Convention that framed the Constitution,) re-enacted substantially the Ordinance of 1787, excluding slavery from the Northwest Territory; and in doing this, nobody dreamed that the Constitution was violated. This being done by the fathers who *made* the instrument, it proves two things, (a) That they did not make the Constitution "to protect" slavery in the Territories, and attached no such meaning to its provisions; (b.) That it was not a violation of that instrument for Congress, acting under it, *to prohibit* slavery in the Territories.

4. The power to prohibit slavery in the Territories has been exercised no less than eleven different times, in addition to those already specified. The exercise of this power began, (so far as authority existed, as shown above,) before the adoption of the Constitution. The acts appear in various periods of our history, and need not be detailed. One of the most important facts in

this connection, is, that as late as the administration of Mr. Polk, a Southern President, with a democratic majority in both Houses of Congress, this power was exercised in the bill for the organization of the Territory of Oregon.

5. The Southern doctrine, therefore, that the Constitution carries slavery into the Territories, and that Congress is bound to "protect" it there by positive law, is a doctrine unrecognized by and unknown to the fathers who made the Constitution, and was never insisted upon by any persons, North or South, until within a comparatively recent period.

Note F.—Page 23.

In view of the facts given in Note E, (above,) is it not a most monstrous perversion of historical truth for Dr. Thornwell to assert, as already quoted from him, that "the Constitution, in its relations to slavery, has been virtually repealed," by the elevation to power of the present administration, where the principle involved is only the securing of the *Territories* to freedom? Read again his statement of the cause of the rebellion, and the ground of his vindication of it: "The presumption clearly is, that there is *something* in the attitude of the Government which PORTENDS danger and demands resistance. There must be a cause for this intense and pervading sense of injustice and of injury. * * * The real cause of the intense excitement of the South, is not vain dreams of national glory in a separate Confederacy, nor the love of the filthy lucre of the African slave-trade; it is the profound conviction that *the Constitution, in its relations to slavery, has been virtually repealed;* that the Government has assumed a *new* and dangerous attitude on this subject; that we have, in short, *new terms of union submitted to our acceptance or rejection.* Here lies the evil. The election of Lincoln, when properly interpreted, is nothing more nor less than a proposition to the South to consent to a Government, *fundamentally different upon the question of slavery from that which our fathers established.* * * * The issue has respect not to the man, but to the principles upon which he is pledged to administer the Government, and which, we are significantly informed, are to be impressed upon it in all time to come. His election seals the triumph of those principles, and that triumph seals the *subversion of the Constitution,* in relation to a matter of paramount interest to the South."

Now, when the historical *facts* are, that in the *earliest* times of the Government, and as *late* as Mr. Polk's administration in 1848, and *so many times* in our history, the action of the Government has been *uniform* in its *positive prohibition* of slavery in the Territories, and *never* has by positive law *protected* it therein, what are we to think of the elaborate statements of Dr. Thornwell in a Quarterly Review, *teaching the contrary of all this?* And yet, such are the men who have instigated and are leading on this rebellion—*for such reasons.*

Note G.—Page 32.

In proof of the point that the Church led the State in the change of views on the merits of the system of slavery, may be cited an article from the *New Orleans True Witness,* a religious paper, edited by Rev. R. McInnis, a Presbyterian clergyman, a native Mississippian, who has the means of knowing whereof he affirms. It is under date of August 18, 1860. It may be added, also, that the Synod of Mississippi officially declare the same thing stated in this article, as to the leading responsibility for this change. The editor remarks as follows:

"SMYLIE ON SLAVERY.—It is an interesting historical fact, that Rev. James Smylie, an old-school Presbyterian minister, was the first person in our country who took boldly the position that slavery was not inconsistent with the teachings of the Bible. He was one of the first Presbyterian ministers who came to the south-west and assisted in forming the Mississippi Presbytery in 1816. The general view held at this time and for many years after, south as well as north, was that slavery was an *evil*. The question had not been examined. All took it for granted that slavery was an evil, and inconsistent with the spirit and teachings of the word of God. Hence the sentiments expressed by our Church, in 1818—which, by the way, has been most shamefully garbled and misrepresented—were at the time the sentiments of the whole country, and was regarded as a pretty strong southern document, hence all the south voted for it. In fact, so strong was the feeling for emancipation that this act of 1818 discouraged it, in our members where the slaves were not prepared for it, while it condemned the "harsh censures and uncharitable reflection" of the more ultra men of the north. We have referred to this merely to call attention to the fact that the opinion of the whole country was that slavery was an evil. And we know of no man who took a different position, until Rev. James Smylie, in answer to a letter addressed to him as stated clerk of the above Presbytery, wrote a reply in which he attempted to show that neither the Old nor the New Testament Scriptures declared slavery to be a sin, but both recognized it as an institution belonging to the great social system. This letter, which has long since been published in a pamphlet of some eighty pages, small type, was not only the first, but it is in our view the ablest and most convincing scriptural argument ever published on the subject. It shows research, ability, honesty, and is unanswerable. When the substance of this letter was delivered in 1835 and '36 in the churches of Mississippi, in the form of a sermon, the people generally, large slave-holders too, did not sympathize with him in his views. We recollect hearing him on one occasion for some three hours, and every person, without exception, thought him somewhat fanatical. The idea that the Bible did sanction slavery was regarded as a new doctrine even in Mississippi. Yet Rev. James Smylie—and a more honest man never lived—was honestly sincere in his convictions and his views, and he went ahead against the tide of public opinion. His scriptural argument has never been answered, nor can it be. This letter was the first thing that turned public attention in the south, and especially in the south-west, to the investigation of the subject; and every scriptural argument we have seen is but a reproduction of this, while none is so clear, full and unanswerable. It ought to be republished.

"Some two years after the publication of this letter, George McDuffie, a senator of South Carolina, announced similar views in Congress, and was regarded there as taking a strange and untenable position—one which met with little sympathy in that body. The fact is, the south had never examined the subject, and were finally driven to it by the intolerant fanaticism of ultra men at the north.

"We mention the above facts, not for the purpose of provoking discussion, but merely to show the state of public opinion at the time on the subject of slavery; and to show that the south is indebted to a minister of our church for the first clear and unanswerable argument against the generally admitted view that slavery was a *sin*."

NOTE II.—PAGE 32.

I have said that the clergy and the church are largely responsible for *leading* in the Southern rebellion. The facts to prove this are abundant. The course of Drs. Palmer and Thornwell, in the earliest days of the movement, are in point. Numerous other cases might be given, but a single significant exhibition must suffice. In the *Southern Presbyterian*, of Columbia, S. C., of April 20, 1861, appears a communication dated Macon, Georgia, entitled "The Church and the Confederate States of America." The editor introduces the writer to his readers thus: "Many of them will recognize it as written by a gentleman occupying a high civil position in the Confederacy, and an Elder in the Presbyterian Church." The communication says: "This revolution has been accomplished *mainly by the Churches.* I do not undervalue the name, and position, and ability of politicians, still I am sure that our success is *chiefly* attributable to the support which they derived from the co-operation of the moral sentiment of the country. Without that, embodying as it obviously did the will of God, *the enterprize would have been a failure.* As a mere fact, it is already historical, that the Christian community sustained it with remarkable unanimity. * * * In times like these upon which we have fallen, the opinion of the Church upon political questions, when unanimously and freely declared, is far more potent than the tricks of the demagogue, or the eloquence of the renowned orator, or the oracular instructions of the retired sage. The reason is, that our Church being sound, has the confidence of the irreligious world. *Let the Church know this, and realize her strength. She should not now abandon* HER OWN GRAND CREATION. She should not leave the creature of her prayers and labors to the contingencies of the times, or the tender mercies of less conscientious patriots. SHE SHOULD CONSUMMATE WHAT SHE HAS BEGUN."

And much more, in this article, to the same effect. Upon the position of the Church as given in this communication, the editor writes his indorsement thus: "We have no fears but that the Christian people of the land will prove faithful to their country in this day of trial, to the very last. As our correspondent suggests, *this present revolution is the result of their uprising.* * * * Much as is due to many of our sagacious and gifted politicians, *they could effect nothing* until the religious union of the North and South was dissolved, *nor until they received the moral support and co-operation of Southern Christians.*"

All this is explicit. The *status* of the Southern clergy and the Southern church in this revolution is fixed by themselves, and acknowledged by Southern politicians. They have assumed the responsibility, and they rejoice in the work of their own hands. *This is history.* What food here for thought, and cause for humiliation, among the people of God!